Do You Really Want a Dog?

Bridget Heos • Illustrated by Katya Longhi

amicus illustrated

Amicus Illustrated is published by Amicus
P.O. Box 1329, Mankato, MN 56002
www.amicuspublishing.us

Library of Congress Cataloging-in-Publication Data

Heos, Bridget.
 Do you really want a dog? / by Bridget Heos ; illustrated by Katya Longhi.
     pages cm. — (Do you really want— ?)
 Includes bibliographical references.
 Summary: "A mischievous dog (and the narrator) teach a young boy the
responsibility—and the joys—of owning a dog. Includes 'Is this pet right for me?'
quiz"—Provided by publisher.
 ISBN 978-1-60753-204-0 (library binding) — ISBN 978-1-60753-395-5 (ebook)
 1. Dogs—Juvenile literature. I. Longhi, Katya, illustrator. II. Title.
 SF426.5.H444 2014
 636.7—dc23
                          2012035930

Editor: Rebecca Glaser
Designer: The Design Lab

Printed in the United States of America at Corporate Graphics
in North Mankato, Minnesota.

Date 11/2015 PO 1276

10 9 8 7 6

About the Author

Bridget Heos is the author of more than
40 books for children and teens, including
What to Expect When You're Expecting Larvae
(2011, Lerner). She lives in Kansas City with
husband Justin, sons Johnny, Richie, and
J.J., plus a dog, cat, and Guinea pig.
You can visit her online at
www.authorbridgetheos.com.

About the Illustrator

Katya Longhi was born in southern Italy.
She studied illustration at the Nemo NT
Academy of Digital Arts in Florence. She loves
to create dream worlds with horses, flying
dogs, and princesses in her illustrations.
She currently lives in northern Italy
with her Prince Charming.

So you say you want a dog.
You really, really want a dog.
But do you _really_ want a dog?

If you have a dog, you'll
need to take him outside
early in the morning.
If you don't…

. . . he'll see everything
as his personal potty.

Next, you'll need to feed him dog food and give him water—two to three times a day. **If you forget...**

. . . he'll eat the trash.
And drink out of the
real toilet.
Poor doggy!

Water doesn't
taste as good in this
doggy bowl.

Do you have a leash?
You'll need to walk him.
If you don't…

. . . he'll burn his energy . . .

GOLD'S
gym

... by turning the whole
house into Dog's Gym!

If you have a puppy, you'll need to play with him lots…and things might get rambunctious! Do you like to run?

Do you like to play fetch for hours?

Do you like tug-of-war?

Great.
I win again.
This is getting
ridiculous.

Your puppy will!
But only if he has
somebody to play with!

You'll have to be serious sometimes, too. Biting
might be cute now...but not when his teeth grow!

Jumping up might be funny now...
but not when he's huge!

Eating off your plate might be good some nights, but not when it's your favorite food.

But doggie treats are okay.

You'll get through this, boy!

No matter how big he gets, he might be afraid of some things…

like going to the vet or taking a bath. But you know these things are good for him!

Lastly, do you like to go places all afternoon—like the park or beach? You'll need to bring puppy with you.

If you leave him home for too long…

Where were you? Oh, and sorry about accidentally destroying the couch.

. . . he'll miss you! And when dogs miss you, they chew!

16

When you're in school, you can leave him in a crate. That will make him feel safe.

But when you get home, he'll be ready to play.
If you don't play with him...

. . . he'll feel lonely. He'll also feel like chewing more things.

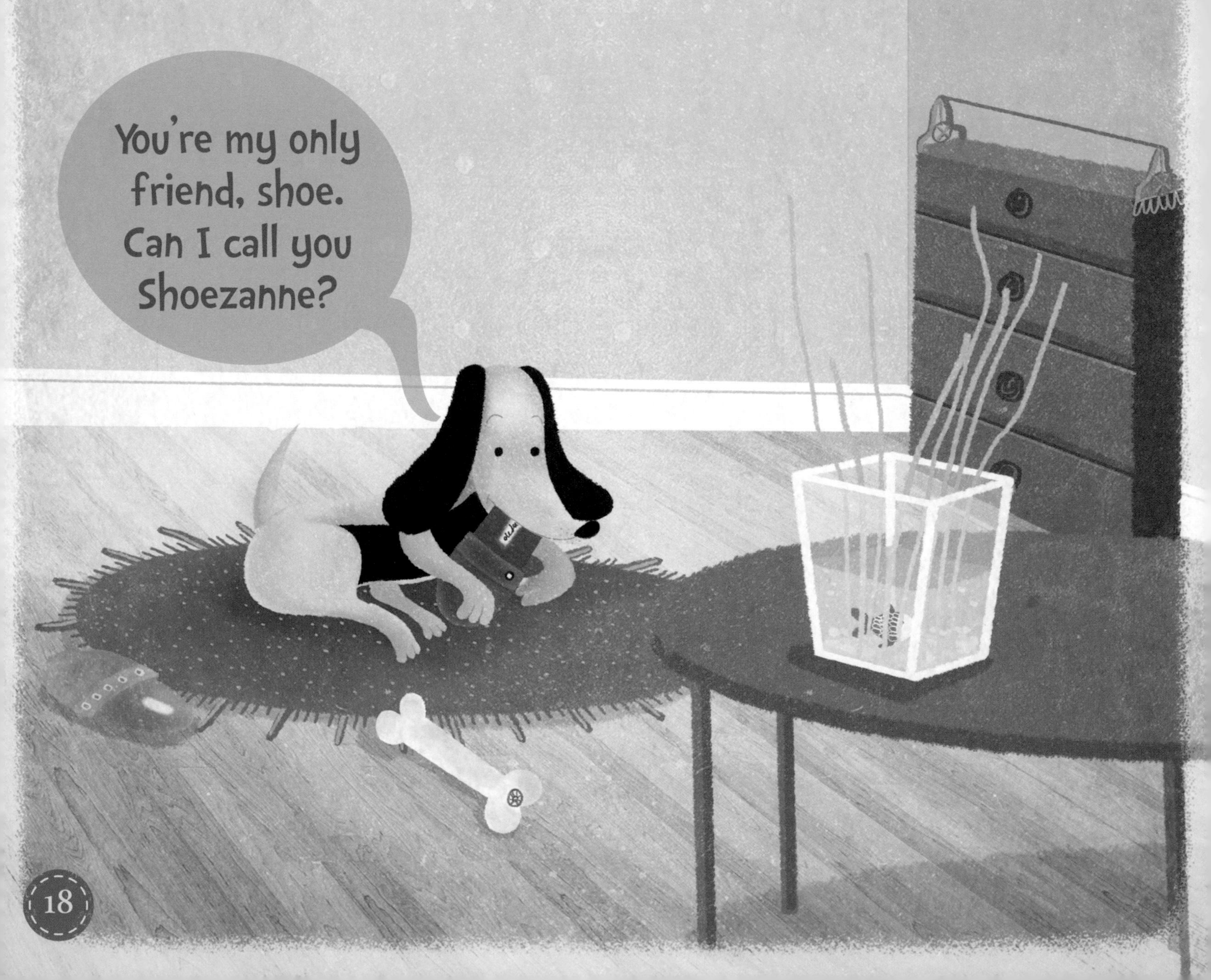

Like you feel when you
have nobody to play with.
(Well, maybe not the shoe part.)
But do you know who will
always play with you?

Your dog!

So if you're willing to feed, water,
bathe, play, and be strict, then maybe
you really do want a dog.

Now I have a question for the dog.
You say you want a person.
You really really want a person.
But do you *really*
want a person?

Of course you do!

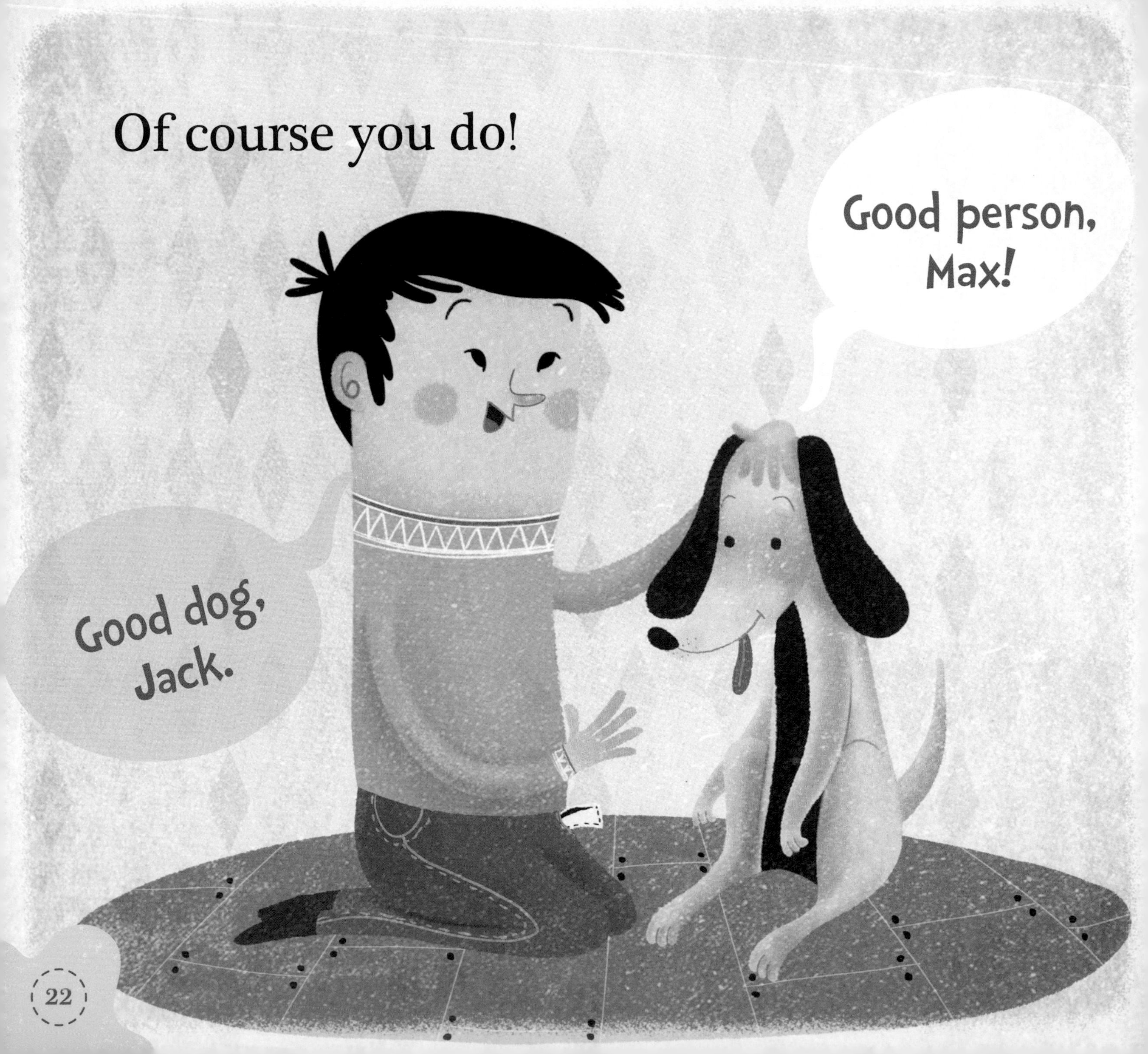

QUIZ

Is this the right pet for me?

Should you get a puppy or an older dog? A little dog or a big dog? And which breed is right for you? Take this quiz to get an idea. (Be sure to talk to breeders or shelter volunteers, too!)

1. Do you have a lot of time to train your dog?
2. Do you have a yard?
3. Do you or your parents have experience training dogs?

If you answered . . .

a. YES TO ALL FOUR QUESTIONS, you can choose almost any type of dog.

b. NO TO NUMBER ONE, you should choose an adult dog that is already trained.

c. NO TO NUMBER TWO, choose a small breed. You'll still need to walk the dog, of course!

d. NO TO NUMBER THREE, choose a breed that is easy to train, such as a Labrador or lab mix. Breeds such as Akitas, German shepherds, and Dobermans can be good dogs but require experienced owners.

Websites

Animal Planet: Guides: Dog Breed Selector
http://animal.discovery.com/breed-selector/dog-breeds.html
Use this interactive online quiz to determine which dog breed is the best fit for your family.

ASPCA Kids
http://www.aspca.org/aspcakids.aspx
The American Society for the Prevention of Cruelty to Animals provides games, photos, and videos that demonstrate pet care, plus information on careers working with animals.

Dog Care and Behavior Tips:
The Humane Society of the United States
http://www.humanesociety.org/animals/dogs/tips/
The Humane Society has advice on dog care, training, and pet adoption.

How to Love Your Dog: A Kid's Guide
http://loveyourdog.com/
Read advice on teaching your dog tricks, how to care for your dog, and find out if you're ready for a dog. Includes videos, photos, and stories submitted by readers.

Tama and Friends visit Petfinder.com
http://www.petfinder.com/tama//index.html
The kids' section of Petfinder.com offers games, pet tips, pet listings, and a section for parents.

Read More

de la Bédoyère, Camilla.
Puppy to Dog. Life Cycles.
QEB Publishing, 2012.

Gaines, Ann Graham.
Top 10 Dogs for Kids.
Enslow Elementary, 2009.

Morgan, Sally.
Dogs. Pets Plus.
Smart Apple Media, 2012.

Wood, Selina.
Owning a Pet Dog. Owning a Pet.
Sea-to-Sea Publications, 2008.

Woof!